PRESS DIONYSUS

2022

First published in 2021 by PRESS DIONYSUS LTD in the UK, 167, Portland Road, N15 4SZ, London.

www.pressdionysus.com

ISBN: 978-1-913961-16-9

ITALY

TRAVELERS STORY BOOK SERIES

Ozlem ISIK

Press Dionysus
ISBN: 978-1-913961-16-9

© 2022 Press Dionysus
First Edition, January 2022, London

Book Design: S. Deniz Akıncı

Press Dionysus LTD, 167, Portland Road, N15 4SZ, London

• e-mail: info@pressdionysus.com
• web: www.pressdionysus.com

ABOUT THE AUTHOR:

The writer, Ms. Ozlem ISIK, has a vast area of expertise in teaching foreign language.

She has both B.A and M.A degrees in teaching a foreign language and has worked in many countries as an ESOL teacher, writer, interpreter and education consultant.

She has developed a unique English learning system and the system has been in use with 100% success rate all over the world.

The writer lives in London, UK, works as an ESOL teacher and she has recently written a story book series called Travelers for ESOL learners and children.

In these stories, the learners will both learn many interesting facts about different countries while travelling with two cute boys named Marcos and Carlo, improve their English language skills and enjoy themselves in a learning process.

ABOUT THE BOOK:

The book is designed and prepared for ESOL learners. In the series which is called Travelers, there are different story books. The learner will comprehend, revise some basic English tenses, structures, phrases and have fun learning amazing facts about various countries in the world.

All learners will travel around the world and learn English at the same time.

This is a first in English teaching; improve your English skills and cultural knowledge.

Don't be sorry!

Read a story...

TRAVELERS STORY BOOK SERIES

Italy

In this chapter, our heroes,
Carlo and Marcos are in

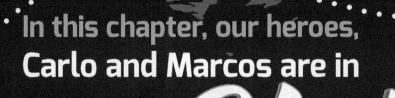

Hi everyone, we are Carlo and Marcos.
We always travel, learn many
interesting, amazing facts about
different countries.
Would you like to join us?

"Our friends want to visit Italy now. It is an amazing country in Southern Europe. The capital city of Italy is Rome."

Marcos was born in Italy and he is the guide in this city tour.

The weather is very nice today in Italy. It is not windy or cold. It is warm and sunny. Marcos and Carlo get up very early in the morning and have a good breakfast. They have some cheese, olives, butter and honey with toasted bread and they drink coffee with milk for breakfast.

They wear hats and sunglasses. They are ready to go out to explore the city. They take their backpacks with them.

hat and sunglasses

explore

Italy is a fascinating country with its rich culture and history.

Here are some amazing facts about the country;

Marcos says;

They have the oldest university in the world. It is "The University of Bologna". The university was founded in 1088.

Italian people like football very much. Juventus is a famous football club in Italy and the club is the winner of the UEFA Champions League twice.

WOW!

There is another very interesting fact here;

Italian police use Lamborghinis, one of the fastest cars in the world.

Italian people are very superstitious.

FRIDAY 13

Examples of some well-known superstitions

For example;

a) If you hear a cat sneeze, it means you can receive good fortune in Italy.

Ahchoo!!!

The number **13** is considered lucky in Italy

You should go...

b) They don't have birds at home because they believe birds bring bad luck.

I'm a good bird!

good

NO GOOD

14

I'm in Italy on New Year's Eve. Don't expect me to dinner.

c) They eat plenty of lentils on New Year's Eve.

d) They never start a journey, new project or get married on a Friday or a Tuesday.

MONDAY

TUESDAY

WEDNESDAY

THURSDAY

FRIDAY

SATURDAY

SUNDAY

e) If you see a spider at night, it is a sign of good income.

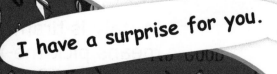

I have a surprise for you.

Friendly

Italian people are very friendly and helpful. You can make lots of Italian friends when you are in Italy.

There is a famous word in Italy, **mommismo.**
It means the attachment between Italian men and their mothers and it is a very big marriage risk in the country.

The average Italian consumes 25 kg of pasta per year.

Tiramisu
(the famous Italian dessert)

The most famous dessert in Italy is tiramisu and it means pick-me-up. Who can resist it?

After learning some facts about the country, our friends want to go to Rome by bus. They go to the bus station and buy their tickets.

On the way to Rome, they start to read some travel guide books. Marcos tries to teach some Italian words to Carlo with no luck☺

Carlo learns the words but forgets them later.

Some famous Italian words are (Please=Per favore, Yes=Si, Buon Giorno=Good morning, Tiamo=I love you...)

Buon Giorno

The Mouth of Truth

Time goes by very quickly and they arrive in Rome. Rome is also called "Caput Mundi" (Capital of the World).

This city must be on everybody's bucket list. It is a very old city. The cats are free to roam in the city. There are many places to visit in Rome. It is also the Eternal City of the world.

Do not forget to visit the "lie detector". "Liar, liar, pants on fire"

The Bocca della Verita (The Mouth of Truth) is a sculpture in the shape of a human face. When you put your hand into the mouth and tell a lie, the sculpture bites the hand.

Liar

Lie Detector

Charity

You should also go and see Trevi Fountain.

Lots of tourists visit the fountain every day and throw a coin into the water. If you do this, it is believed that you can visit Rome again. Then the money is collected from the fountain and given to the charity named Caritas. The charity helps poor people in the city.

When visiting the city, you do not need to buy water because there are a lot of fountains in the city. You can go to the fountains and drink water.

Man Gladiator   **Woman Gladiator**

Their next stop is the famous Collosseum monument in Rome. It is a symbol of Italy and one of the main tourist attractions. It was the scene of the fights between gladiators and wild animals just for public amusement.

The gladiators were usually slaves, prisoners of war or criminals. They were not men only. There were women gladiators as well. The Colosseum is a symbol of Human Rights and death penalty now.

The weather is hot and sunny in Rome and Marcos and Carlo want to eat ice cream because Italian ice cream, gelato, is the best ice cream in the world.

Italian Ice Cream, Gelato

Sunny

They go to the Spanish Steps to meet some of their friends. "The Spanish Steps" is used as a meeting place. People go there to relax and take a break. There are 135 steps there. "The Spanish Steps" was also the scene of an old movie "Roman Holiday" (1953)

Cupid with his bow

Rome is the city of romance. If you reverse the word Roma "the Italian word for Rome", you get "Amor"- meaning love.

Marcos and Carlo are very happy in Italy. They hope you also liked it.

See you in another country soon.

B.B.F.N.
(Bye-bye for now)

EXERCISES

ANSWER THE QUESTIONS

1) What is the capital city of Italy?

- - - - -

2) Who is the guide in the city tour? Why?

- - - - -

3) What do they have for breakfast?

- - - - -

4) What is the famous football club in Italy? Which team do you support in your country?

- - - - -

5) Are Italian people superstitious? If so, give two examples? Do you have any superstitions? What are they?

- - - - -

6) What is the famous Italian dessert? Do you have a favourite dessert? What is it?

- - - - -

7) How do they go to Rome?

- - - - -

8) Do you remember some of the places to visit in Italy? Give two examples.

- - - - -

1) If you put a coin into the _____, you can return to Rome one day.

2) What do you want to do before you die? What is on your _____?

3) In some countries people do not use number 13. They believe it brings bad luck. These people are _____.

4) He likes to _____ old caves to learn more about ancient times in Rome.

5) They decided to get married after 90 minutes, It was a real _____.

6) The _____ aims to help poor people.

7) Most students carry _____ to school.

8) The Grand Canyon is a famous _____ in the States.

9) When a mother gives birth to her child, it is an example of an _____.

10) _____ Day is celebrated annually across the world on 10 December every year.

LIST:

fountain, bucket list, charity, tourist attraction, Human Rights, romance, explore, backpacks, superstitious, attachment

1) A: _?

B: Tiramisu is the famous Italian dessert.

2) A: _?

B: Carlos was born in Italy.

3) A: _?

B: Yes, Italian people like football.

4) A: _?

B: It is warm and sunny today.

5) A: _?

B: They drink coffee with milk for breakfast.

LIST:

UK, Turkey, Spain, Italy, USA, New Zealand, Germany, Canada

E   MAKE A SHORT LIST OF THE ITALIAN SUPERSTITIONS

F   WRITING ACTIVITY

Write a short paragraph about the superstitions in your country and compare it with the ones in Italy.